OLD POLISH LEGENDS

OLD POLISH LEGENDS

RETOLD BY

F. C. ANSTRUTHER

WOOD-ENGRAVINGS BY

J. SEKALSKI

FOREWORD BY

Z. NOWAKOWSKI

HIPPOCRENE BOOKS, INC.
New York

For information, address:
HIPPOCRENE BOOKS, INC.
171 Madison Avenue
New York, NY 10016

ISBN 0-87052-023-7

Printed in the United States of America.

M 9 8 7 6 5 4 3 2 1

CONTENTS

FOREWORD

IN the evening, when the wind howls outside the windows, when the rain beats against the panes and the logs are crackling on the hearth, you must strain your ears, order everyone to be silent and wait patiently for a gentle knock on the door. One scarcely hears the delicate tap for there is nothing of importunity about it. A Fairy-tale is knocking. You must open the door wide to her and seat her near the fireplace, so that she may warm herself and rest awhile. For after all she has come from far off, from beyond the seven mountains, from beyond the seven rivers. Drenched with rain, chilled in the autumn gale, she is perhaps hungry and thirsty. You must give her food and drink, you must comfort her, for as soon as she is at rest she will begin to speak, to talk, to talk without ceasing, to recall the ancient, beautiful times, to laugh and to weep.

Reader, draw close this Polish Fairy-tale. On hearing her gentle tap, open the door, seat her near the fire and wait until she begins to speak. She will not take up much room, a crumb of bread offered with an open hand, a drop of water, the warmth of the fireside, will suffice. This is a Polish Fairy-tale. She has crossed more than seven rivers, more than seven mountains, and they were rivers and mountains red with blood. She will tell what she has to tell and then she will continue on her way. She, alone in the world, is a homeless, wandering Fairy-tale, who walks barefoot, singing to herself and to the people.

Shelter her for a moment, British reader. You will hear the legend of a Polish Princess, who, rather than wed a German, threw herself into the waves of the Vistula. You will hear the tale of the wise king who slew a terrible dragon. You will hear the tale of the white eagle, whose snowy feathers were reddened with blood, and hearing this tale you will understand why the Poles have in their crest an eagle, white as snow, on a field as red as blood. A lovely tale!

But you will also hear others. The wind will howl and beat against the panes, the rain will sing, the logs will crackle in the hearth, while this Fairy-tale, walking barefoot from beyond a hundred rivers, from beyond a hundred mountains, will enlighten you as to why, for example, a melody which is known to you and which Polish trumpeters play, breaks off on a certain hair-fine, but unfinished note. She, this barefoot and homeless Fairy-tale, will explain this sudden break in the melody, which is known to many Scottish towns, and, indeed, to many English towns.

Ah! What an extraordinary story this is! Seven hundred years ago a guard on the top of the tower of St. Mary's Church in Cracow caught sight of the Tartar hordes advancing from afar, sounded the alarm and roused the sleeping town, but suddenly a Tartar arrow pierced his throat ere he had finished the tune, which from that time onwards for seven hundred years suddenly breaks off violently on a note as high as the heavens.

A lovely tale! But this is only half of it, for the continuation is sung to Cracow by distant Samarkand, the seat of the great Mongol powers of Timur or Tamerlaine. In 1941, when Polish soldiers, freed from Russian prisons, barefoot and hungry like our Fairy-tale to-day, reached Samarkand and played this song, or Marjacki "Hejnal," the dwellers in the capital of Uzbekistan were filled with wonder. They listened and listened, and when the melody was suddenly broken the old people recalled a certain age-old prophecy which proclaims that when the sons of Lechistan, or in other words Poles, shall some day come to Samarkand and sing this strange song in the square, then Uzbekistan will regain its freedom.

This is indeed an unusual tale, which across nearly half the world and across seven hundred years unites two foreign nations. Is this now the end of the legend of the Cracow "Hejnal"? One cannot tell. Wherever, during this War, the foot of the Polish soldier has halted, there this same melody has resounded. It is known to Monte Cassino, to Tobruk, lying in the sands of Libya, to snow-covered Narwik in Norway, to many French, Dutch, Belgian and German towns. Many Scottish and English towns know this unfinished melody. Perhaps some day, some day when we shall no longer be here, those towns will sing the continuation of it. Perhaps they will unravel the end of this broken melody, as fine as a thread? Perhaps in numerous towns, after many, many years, when outside the window the wind and rain are moaning, the aged will relate to the children round the fireside the story of the Poles who used to be here but who went far off to their own free land, leaving behind them only a memory, sometimes faint, sometimes cut short like the melody of the "Hejnal." . . .

Should one believe in fairy tales? Are all fairy tales true? All, but only on one condition: they must be beautiful. I am a Pole, but I am writing this foreword to a collection of tales recorded by an authoress who wished to give shelter to a Polish Fairy-tale, to open her home wide to her, to invite her into the circle round the fire, to give her food and drink. The authoress is not a Pole, but she took great pains to master our strange language, to learn our peculiar history, to delve deep into the realm of fairy tales connected with a far-off land, lying beyond a hundred bloody rivers, beyond a hundred equally bloody mountains. I believe there came to the authoress' help, besides a strong will, the realisation that this homeless, barefooted Polish Fairy-tale is the tale of Freedom, of that priceless gift which should be the right of each and every nation. To save the freedom of her country Princess Wanda, "who desired no German," threw herself into the waves of the Vistula, to-day one of the bloodiest rivers in the world.

One must believe in all fairy tales, for all are true, on this one condition, however, that they must be beautiful. Now, the narratives contained in the present modest collection fully comply with this condition. They are beautiful, very beautiful. And in them, as in fairy tales throughout the world, all kings are valiant, all knights gallant, all princesses lovely, all horses swift and unsurpassed, every goblet is of pure gold, every sword of steel, every heart warm and eager. Also, in them, as in all fairy tales throughout the world, Good always conquers and Evil suffers a well-deserved punishment.

Scientific enquirers into legends and myths tell us that there is not even the most fantastic, the most improbable legend, which has not some slight foundation in real facts. In other words, in every legend there is a spark of truth. In short, it is somewhat similar with legends as with old proverbs. They are not only the wisdom and property of individual nations, but in fact they represent equally the wisdom and eternal property of the whole of mankind. Thus, a Pole, for example, would be inclined to swear that—let us take whatever comes first to mind—the proverb about the gift horse is genuinely and exclusively a Polish proverb, because from time immemorial we have said *"Darowanemu koniowi nie zaglada sie w zeby"*—"Never look a gift horse in the mouth." But the average Italian will strike his breast and maintain that none other than the sons of Italy forged the proverb "Al' cavall' donato non si guarda in bocca." A German, in true German fashion, after hearing the Polish and Italian versions, will say decisively and with complete certainty that it comes from beyond the Rhine, that it is another version of the German "Dem geschenkten Gaul schaut man nicht ins Maul." And meanwhile the learned enquirer, listening to that German, will only smile and whisper that there is nothing new under the sun, that the ancient Greeks already showed wisdom in their proverbs and that they used to say, for instance, "He who sows in a wind, reaps in a storm." . . .

Similarly, legends, or at any rate the greater part of them, came into existence earlier than would seem possible to us. If the Polish Prince, Krakus, killed the legendary dragon, this monster must have been quite a near relation of the Sphinx, which devoured the inhabitants of a town older than Cracow, namely Teb, the capital of Beocia. If Oedipus was forced to solve riddles and was threatened with death if he did not find a solution, let us remember that under another sky, in another clime, the beautiful Princess Turandot also set her lovers difficult riddles and in the event of being unable to solve them the audacious young man put his head under the executioner's axe. If the mythical Daedalus stuck wings on to himself and his son so that they might escape from imprisonment—in every latitude, among all peoples, we find this same tale, a tale as old as the yearning common to every man, the yearning which urges him not to walk upon the earth but to soar above the clouds.

Are legends true? Certainly! We Poles have, for instance, a story about a mountain brigand in the Tatra or Pieniny Mountains, who built himself a strange kind of aeroplane, and in it flew away beyond the sky. However, besides this legend, we have another recorded story, which is not only lightly based on reality, but which is indeed firmly founded on facts and can be proved exactly with dates, names, &c., and yet tells of a Daedalus constructing the first Polish aeroplanes at the Court of King Wladyslaw IV.

In Berlin in 1682 a certain Dr. J. J. Becher published a book which tells of different "Mechanische und Merkantilische Concepten und Praepositionen," quoting the account given by the English Ambassador at the Court of Warsaw, Mr. Simon, about the first airman in Poland. With the help of an apparatus constructed of straw and rushes, he had raised himself into the air, although during his flight "es hat allezeit etwas gefehlt"—there was always something lacking. But more important than those not very successful experiments was the project for the introduction of permanent air communication between Warsaw and Constantinople—let us add, however, that for the flight between these two towns, quite distant from each other, they allowed—12 hours. A reckless idea! And let us also note that that project arose in the first half of the 17th century! Here indeed the ancient Greek myth of Daedalus meets the truth of the 20th century!

Apparently our King proved to be generous towards the inventor and poured forth zlotys like ducats in a fairy tale. Almost at the same time, and strictly speaking even a few score years earlier, a native Daedalus appeared in Russia. He was an ordinary peasant, a Russian "muzhik," to whom, in the reign of Ivan the Terrible, came the desire to fly into the sky. The nobles found out about this daredevil, dragged him off to Moscow and arranged a demonstration. The poor wretch apparently flew over the roofs of several houses, but when the Tsar heard about this experiment he ordered Daedalus to be impaled, so that the peasants' heads would not be turned. They are to walk on the ground.

These are two similar episodes, illustrating the fact that the legend of the man who wished to fly is common to all peoples. The ending alone is different. In Poland ducats, in Russia the stake! When in Rome do as Rome does!

I enlarged a little more upon this fairy tale, which is the incontestable property of all ages and all peoples, because in Great Britain the best known section of the Polish Armed Forces is our Air Force. I believe that the memory of them, of the defenders of London at the time of the Battle of Britain, will remain longer, perhaps even one day will grow into a legend. It will be a homeless fairy tale about homeless knights fighting for other people's homes.

The legends contained in the present collection omit Warsaw, although the engraving on the cover correctly represents the coat of arms of the capital of Poland—a mermaid. These legends speak almost exclusively of Gniezno and Cracow. It is, therefore, my duty here to exonerate the authoress and in a certain sense to complete her small collection. Certain characters, appearing in these legends, belong to history, namely to the oldest period recorded in our annals, of which the first date is the year 963. Mieszko, Boleslaw the Brave, St. Wojciech, Otton III, all of these are people who actually lived and worked, about whom we know a great deal from early records, from ancient annals and chronicles. Other characters, such as for instance Piast or Lech, descend from that epoque in which history seems as if she is fondling her snow-white quill, not yet dipped in the ink. She dips it in the ink-pot and sets it down on a sheet of parchment, I repeat, in the year 963.

Why then such silence about Warsaw, which not only lies in the geometric centre of Europe, but lies equally in the centre of Poland? At that time the future capital of our State is a small village, a fishing settlement on the banks of the Vistula and is only just beginning to dream a dream of the future great career which awaits her. Even in the year 1281 two Masovian Dukes, one dwelling in Plock and the other in Czersk, are carrying on a quarrel not about Warsaw but about nearby Jazdy, because Warsaw simply does not come into the picture at all. I gave the date of that quarrel in order to compare it with some other date, for instance with one concerning Florence: in 1280 Florence has 45,000 inhabitants, rich merchants, craftsmen, bankers, &c. On the other hand, Warsaw at that time has perhaps 100 inhabitants, poor fishermen, or perhaps even fewer. At the outbreak of this War Florence had over 300,000 inhabitants, Warsaw 1,300,000. Not in vain did Ferdinand Lesseps, creator of the Suez Canal, a town-planner of the first water, foresee a magnificent future for Warsaw as the town which lies at the point of intersection of two straight lines stretching from the extreme north and south, east and west, of Europe. There on the Vistula all roads cross, there is the heart of Europe.

But to-day Warsaw's heart is pierced. Warsaw represents the peak of the world's Golgotha. In Warsaw intersect all high tension lines bearing the greatest load of pain and heroism. And her legends? Warsaw has comparatively few legends, not fairy tales but history lulled her to sleep. That very history which is reborn in a legend. Nevertheless, to-day when I am writing the foreword to a volume of Polish fairy tales, I will open the scanty treasury of Warsaw legends in order to obtain from it a pearl of exceptional splendour and unusual brilliancy.

But before I take the plunge and draw a deep breath in order to recount this legend, I must in all honesty state that similar or practically similar legends also belong to other, not necessarily Polish, towns. The Warsaw legend, however, is distinguished by exceptional accuracy, it is based on dates and a host of names and facts, by reason of which it undoubtedly seems to stand above similar narratives of which other towns boast.

Incipiam! At the time when the wave of the Reformation had rolled across Europe, a Warsaw merchant, Jurga, a descendant of the powerful family of Baryczka, set out on a journey to Germany and happened to come to Nuremburg, where he witnessed the destruction of churches, altars, holy books and effiigies of Christ. That night Jurga had a vision: his forefather, the blessed Martin Baryczka, appeared to him, ordered him to get up immediately, dress himself, go out into the town and find and take to Warsaw a figure of Christ, of which the neck, arms and legs had been broken off by the heretics. The merchant fulfilled this command. He succeeded in finding the figure, covered with mud and ashes. He washed it in wine, wrapped it in a white cloth and placed it in one of his wagons. On the way to Poland bandits attacked Jurga's caravan, but as soon as they touched the wagon in which the Christ was hidden their hands were withered. The merchant safely reached Warsaw, carried the figure to the Cathedral and ordered a wood-carver to remake the limbs which had been broken off.

Here begins the most beautiful and deeply moving chapter of the story: after the carver, Maciej from Pniew, had finished his work, it was the turn of the joiner, a certain Bialowas. He had begun to nail the Christ to a new Cross when suddenly from the hands and feet of the Saviour dripped blood, living, warm blood. The people flocked there, the whole of Warsaw crowded into the Cathedral, but the miracle did not end here, for in the course of one night the Christ's hair grew, so luxuriant and long that each year it was necessary to cut it so that it would not cover His face. We know the names of people who were cured by the miraculous Christ of "The Dark Chapel" of the Warsaw Cathedral. We even know that the golden scissors with which they performed the cutting of the hair each year were once the property of Anna, the last Masovian Princess, we know many details of this mystery, which took place each year. . . .

Should one believe in legends? One must if they are beautiful, and this legend of the Christ of "The Dark Chapel" is very beautiful and worthy of the town which is honoured with it. From inanimate wood gushes fresh warm blood. In the course of one night luxuriant young hair grows afresh. To us homeless Poles, when we are unable to sleep at night, this legend now comes on silent, bleeding feet and knocks, saying: "Open and believe! I come from Warsaw! From the town whose neck, arms and legs they cut off in September, 1939, but who, notwithstanding, arose four years later! I come from Warsaw, whose inhabitants leapt once more into the struggle on the 1st September, 1944! From Warsaw, which never loses hope, from Warsaw which is like wood, dead in appearance, and yet is full of living sap and ardent blood. From Warsaw, which springs forth anew, luxuriant and young like the hair of the Christ of "The Dark Chapel." Admit me, allow me to rest a moment, to warm myself, let me eat and drink my fill and in return for this I will begin to tell you about the town where Freedom has been hidden deep below the ground, to come out into the light of day only when the time is ripe!"

When the autumn wind howls outside the windows, when the rain beats against the panes, when the logs are crackling on the hearth, you must strain your ears, order everyone to be silent and wait patiently until a faint, delicate knock is heard. It is the knock of a Fairy-tale from beyond the seven rivers, from beyond the seven mountains. The Polish Fairy-tale knocks still more quietly, because she comes barefooted and homeless, from beyond a hundred bloody rivers, from beyond a hundred bloody mountains. She has torn and bleeding feet, and yet she is not always sad, but she is always beautiful. All her kings are valiant, all knights gallant, all princesses lovely, all horses are swift and unsurpassed, but the eagle in this fairy tale is as white as snow, on a field as red as blood.

ZYGMUNT NOWAKOWSKI.

THE LEGEND OF LECH AND GNIEZNO

MANY, many years ago, even many centuries ago, there lived in Polish lands a Duke named Lech. It was long, long ago, and some say it was even before the time of Alexander the Great. Be that as it may, in the land of Poland there was as yet no town of Poznan, nor of Kruszwica, nor were there any large cities in Greater Poland. The country was wild, with few people; men lived together in small communities, greatly fearing the savage Goths who invaded them from the west and the wild Huns who came in from the east. Death and desolation came in the wake of these invaders, and the peaceful, agricultural Slavs were obliged to become warriors, that they might defend their homes and families from destruction.

Lech was the first Duke of Poland. He it was who first established a Dukedom on the soil of Poland and assumed the leadership of the western Slavs. He united the tribes, and from the time of his reign, Poland developed and grew prosperous. Better strongholds were built to resist the raids of the savage neighbours, the fields were tilled and hides were cured, and with the arrival of more settled times, men grew more civilised and turned to the making of pottery, agricultural implements and furniture, the pattern and style of which has changed but little, and even to-day utensils can be seen in use, very similar to those which were used in the time of Lech.

In order to ensure the defence of his country against invasion, Lech kept a strong army. This was well-equipped, well trained and vast. It covered itself with glory and indeed the name of Lech, its captain, became so famous throughout the world, that his fiefs were called Lechici, and the Muscovites often called the Poles Lachi, and the Turks named Poland Lechistan, or the country of Lech. His power stretched over so wide an area of country that the Hungarian Lengyel also almost certainly comes from Lech.

The Duke was in every way an outstanding man. He was very tall and broad shouldered, and such was his strength that he could wield a battleaxe which ordinarily took two men to lift. He was handsome, with fair hair, blue eyes and well-defined, acquiline features. Not only was he a fearless warrior, he was also a wise ruler and, unlike most men of his stamp, had a taste for learning. He had this in common with most princes: he loved hunting, and his leisure was generally devoted to the sport. As in battle, he led the field, and always claimed the first stroke at bear or boar, when the beast was brought to bay. He had a true, brave heart and valued courage in another, be it man or beast.

Lech also loved falconry, and had many goshawks and peregrine falcons, some of which he had trained himself. He had tried to train a young buzzard, but the bird, after giving great promise, had died. The Duke had expressed the wish to train an eagle, and though his falconers had advised him that it was impossible, he still persisted in hoping that he might capture and train a young golden eagle, for he thought that it would be swifter and stronger, in the flight after its quarry, than any goshawk.

One fine spring day, the Duke and his court went hawking. A goodly company set forth from the castle, each one mounted and each dressed in the green hunting habit which Lech had commanded should be worn by all those who joined the chase with him. The Duke rode at the head of the cavalcade, with his favourite hawk on his wrist, closely followed by his Master of the Hunt. He seemed to be in thoughtful mood, and paid little heed to the conversation which was taking place around him. Then, without preamble, he gave his bird to the Master of the Hunt, saying curtly, "I would be alone"; and, setting spurs to his horse, he galloped off. His company were surprised and troubled, but no man attempted to follow the Duke, for sometimes he was given to strange moods and at such times it was better not to approach him.

Lech urged his steed forward, he knew not why, but feeling an irresistible desire to reach a hill which he espied in the distance. After galloping a while, he reached it, and, reining in his steed, looked around him. At first he could discern nothing, but soon he perceived a nest, perched on a rocky crag. It was the nest of a white eagle, who sat with her young around her. She was a noble bird, with curved beak and powerful talons, and wings to bear her aloft in strong and graceful flight. This was the

eagle that Lech had dreamed to possess; this was the bird which would make falcony a delight, which would rouse the envy of every prince in Europe and beyond. He resolved to capture one of the young, take it home to his castle, and train it with all the care and skill at his command. What a rare prize this would be! What pleasure lay in store for him if he could but obtain one of those eaglets!

He leapt from his horse and climbed towards the nest. The white eagle watched him intently, while her fledgelings, surprised by the approach of a stranger, crept under her wings. Lech shouted and waved his arms, thinking to frighten the bird from her nest, but she stirred not. The Duke came nearer, and put forth his hand, and the eagle, with a swift movement, pecked at him as though in warning. But Lech heeded her not. Reaching for his dagger, he held it aloft, so that the bird must wound herself if she approached him too near. With his other hand, he again attempted to grasp one of the eaglets, but the mother-bird was upon him once more and this time, neither prince nor bird escaped unscathed. Lech persisted; he ardently longed for one of the eaglets and was loath to abandon a prize which he thought he could capture with ease. The struggle continued. Lech, using his dagger more freely, was making desperate attempts to approach the nest. But he was beaten off by the sharp beak and powerful wings of the mother. The eagle had been wounded several times, and blood was staining the white feathers with dark, crimson splashes. She defended her nest and her freedom and the liberty of her little ones. The Duke's brave and generous heart was touched by this unyielding defence and by this noble courage, and the sight of the blood which trickled down the bird's white breast made him ashamed of his desire to deprive of its freedom the offspring of so valiant a mother. He turned away abruptly, and descended the hill, deep in thought. A brave bird, who spilt her blood for her freedom and for that of her eaglets!

Then Lech sat down at the foot of the hill and looked at the scene before him. As far as his eye could reach stretched the fair lands of Poland, his country that he loved with all his heart. Would he not defend her, just as the eagle had defended her nest? And the thought came to him: let that brave, white eagle become the badge of Poland, let her be the token of freedom for which all those worthy of the name of Pole should shed their blood, and the eagle's blood be the symbol of bravery. Poland is immortal; so shall the White Eagle be immortal. Thus to this day, on the shield and banner of Poland, is blazoned the white eagle on a crimson field.

And the place was pleasing to the Prince. He loved that hill where he had found the eagle's nest and which still bears his name. He took his counsellors to the spot and showed it to them, saying, "Let us build our nests here, as do the eagles"! So a castle was built, and then a city, and it was called "Gniezno," which, in the Polish of those days, meant "nest." And in those far-off times Gniezno became a fair city, and was the capital of Lech's Dukedom, lying on the hillside which bears his name.

The White Eagle has always been on the banners of Poland and when, as has occured many times, Poland has been attacked, her sons have defended her no less bravely than the eagle who long ago shed her blood in the defence of freedom.

THE STORY OF POPIEL, WHO WAS EATEN BY
THE MICE

BESIDE the Lake of Goplo, in the town of Kruszwica, to this day, stand the ruins of an ancient castle. Only one tower remains untouched by the hand of time, and it stands alone, pointing towards Heaven like an accusing finger. It is a beautiful tower, made of bricks, which centuries have mellowed into a silvery pink, and it rises gracefully from the highest point of Kujawia's rolling, green plain. If you go right to the top of that tower, which is called the Tower of the Mice, you will have an arduous climb up steep, spiral stairs, but you will be rewarded, when you reach the height, by the beauty which will greet your eyes. There, below you, will be the fair fields of Poland. Far, far away they stretch, as far as the eye can see, beautiful in their fertility, noble in their broad expanse. Beneath the tower, cherry trees and apple grow among the ruins of the old castle, making it gaudy with their blossom in the spring, whereas in summer it becomes the favourite haunt of the children of Kruszwica. The town itself is small to-day, and unimportant, but it is neat and clean and bears itself proudly, as though conscious of its famous, historic past. To the north of the town stands the Parish Church, built in Gothic. On one of the walls of the Church you will see the portrait, roughly and inexpertly limned, of Bishop Marcin Gall, who was the anonymous chronicler of the times of Boleslaw the Wry-mouthed. He it was who first wrote of Polish history, who first related the Polish legends. We owe a great debt to the good Bishop, for thanks to his scholarly pen many facts about early Polish history have been preserved, which would otherwise have been lost in the mists of the past.

To the South of Kruszwica lies the Lake of Goplo which mirrors the trees that grow around it in its tranquil waters. It is a long, narrow lake, and it stretches towards the south, reflecting the blue sky in its glancing waters, mirroring the last golden rays of the setting sun. Sometimes the winds ruffle its placid face and then its waves are irridescent and rain-

bow hued. To the east and west of the lake are verdant fields which sweep away to the horizon, and sway in summer, silver and gold, as the breeze ripples, with a gentle sigh and a whisper through the ripening corn. Here and there are orchards, over which can be seen the wooden roofs of farms and villages, like islands in a sea of pink and white blossom. There are manor houses too, whose roofs are taller, and which are approached by avenues of poplars. These always seem to be centres of great activity. Far away, lost in the mist, is the southern shore of Goplo. It reaches away into the horizon, to beyond Inowroclaw, to Pakosc, even to Trzemeszno.

The country was dotted here and there with watch-towers, from the heights of which the citizens would scan the sky-line for any sign of the approaching foe. Some of these still stood until recent years, but the latest and most cruel of all wars has doubtless destroyed the last of these age-old landmarks.

As you stand, lost in contemplation of this lovely country, a little awed, perhaps, by the beauty around you, the sound of music may fall upon your ears. Voices, if it is the month of May, will be singing hymns in praise of the Most Blessed Virgin, Queen of Poland. You will realise you are in Poland, in the very cradle of that Polish Kingdom which was built up by the strong hands of the Piast dynasty which took over the rule after the Popiels had perished. They ruled over the tribe of Polanie or Polans* who settled here and assumed the leadership of other tribes, whose princes were subordinate to them. The Polanie built powerful Poland and a united Polish nation.

Imagine then, that you are standing on the summit of the Tower of the Mice and I will tell you the history of that Tower.

.   .   .   .

It happened in the Ninth Century. Prince Lech and his capital of Gniezno were only memories in the minds of men, as a story their grand-fathers had heard from their grandfathers. There were some old people who remembered Leszek I and Leszek II. The capital had been removed from Gniezno to Kruszwica, and there reigned the second and last Popiel.

---

*Polanie were the strongest Polish tribe, the name comes from pole (field), on which they settled, as distinct from other tribes who lived in the woods or marshes, on the Vistula or in Silesia.

He was the worst and most cruel of all Polish kings and princes, and perhaps only Waclaw, King of Bohemia and Poland, who "wept, did penance and murdered in turn," could be compared with him, though no one could match him in cunning and deceit. It cannot be that Polish blood flowed in his veins, for how could such wickedness be found in a Pole?

Bishop Marcin Gall gives him the Latin name of "Choscius." Some say that his name was "Chwostek," which in old Slavonic means "Little Tail." But others think rather, that his name was not "Chwost" ("Tail"), but "Chwast," which signifies "Weed." In truth he was akin to those bad weeds which grew in such abundance on the lands of Poland, which men were obliged to uproot, and quickly, lest they should poison the soil. His official name was Popiel II.

He lived in the castle of Kruszwica, for he did not like the old Gniezno of Lech. He was not satisfied with a stronghold made of wood, as were other Polish Kings and Princes, who lived according to the old, Slavonic customs. Their castles were crowned with wooden towers, surrounded by stout wooden palisades, and they all had a moat. You would think this was sufficient for anyone, but no: Chwast must have his castle made of brick, after the German fashion. He thought that he was safer in a castle built of brick and he also thought that he would be quite secure, even if the people should revolt against his wicked ways. So German artisans came, and built the castle of Kruszwica, of brick, in the German fashion. The townspeople were not pleased at the irruption of these strangers, who were loud, bold and quarrelsome. They drank far too much, and swaggered around the town as though it were their own. But they were clever workmen, and they built Popiel such a castle as had never been seen before. It was strong, and beautiful, with a wide moat and several fine towers, and nothing was spared to make the interior as luxurious as the exterior was massive.

The castle pleased Chwastek's wife, who was a German woman. She was very beautiful, but she was very wicked, even more wicked and cunning than Popiel himself. But she was beautiful, tall, slender, red-haired, with slanting, green eyes and a red and lustful mouth. She was a bad woman, and used her beauty for evil ends. She was a German. Her name I cannot now recall, though I have heard it. Perhaps it was Ortrud, or Krimhilda, or even something more outlandish than that. It is enough that she was wicked, red-haired and German. In appearance Popiel was a strong contrast to his wife. He was fat, with a pink face, small eyes and loose, moist lips. He had a fleshy nose and a rather receding forehead, and his fair hair was conspicuously sparse. But he was tall, and his presence could command respect. The only beautiful feature he possessed was his hands, which, strangely enough, were long, thin and white. But, looking closely at them, you could see that they were mean, grasping hands, more like claws than the hands of a man.

The royal couple thought of nothing except amusement, licence and extravagance. They imposed ruinous taxation on the people to pay for the orgies at the castle. They ordered that all the skins from the forests, all the fish from the rivers, all the beasts from the farms, and all the honey from the hives should be brought to them. They seized everything for themselves and left their people destitute. To plunder merchants and even guests was their chief delight. And they were licentious. No maiden was safe from the amorous attentions of the King, the fairest were all with child by him. The youths of the city were brought under guard to the castle, in order that they might satisfy the desires of the queen. The nation was ruined. The people were starving and unhappy. To seek justice was useless. Those who approached the castle hoping to do so were either thrown to the dogs, or locked in a cage, unarmed, with a bear. The King and Queen watched the struggles of the wretched victims of their cruelty with delight. Merchants were not only plundered, but thrown into a dungeon, among serpents and rats, where they remained until ransom should be paid for them.

Popiel coveted the goods of others. He seized the lands belonging to his own uncles, he stole their cattle, he burned their castles, he pillaged their estates and brought back the booty to Kruszwica. He must have everything for his pleasures. His food must be perfect, his wine must be spiced to his taste, otherwise, he would fly into an uncontrollable rage. He loved foreign spices, saffron, pepper and cinamon. His jaded, over-pampered palate demanded spices, everything that he ate or drank must be spiced to satisfy the senses which had been dulled and satiated by excess. He spent nights in orgies which were marked by unrestrained licence, he loved to watch dancing, but dancing of the wildest kind. If he could find gipsies, he would carry them off to his castle and make them dance their wild, graceful dances until they fell, exhausted, on the floor of the banqueting-hall. When he was drunk he would even shoot arrows at his own servants, and many a lad was wounded or killed for his master's pleasure. He loved hunting too, but he was not content with the sport. He would range the countryside, riding over farmlands, through orchards, scattering and killing flocks and herds. He delighted in setting fire to the villages, in destroying the property of others, in witnessing their tears and misery. This was his great amusement. If he could provoke tears of anger, of sorrow, of real misery, then he would be content. He was a real German.

All men hated Popiel, deep in their hearts, and they meditated revenge. But what could they do? Popiel was so securely guarded by his armed courtiers, who served him like faithful dogs, that it was impossible to approach him. These men, hard-hearted like their master, rough and warlike, were called "my vikings" by the King. They did not understand kindness, and their devotion to their master was perhaps rather on account of the good living which they enjoyed in his service, than from any especial love which they bore him. But there was good food, and plenty, drink in abundance and high pay. So they ate, drank, wenched and lived like lords. And they always wore chain mail on their breasts.

The people, driven to desperation, sometimes tried to revolt. They would march on the castle, but such a castle was not to be conquered, nor yet burned down. For it was built of brick. And then Chwastek would appear. He would dress himself in his armour, seize a large battle-axe and face the prisoners who had been taken in the action. After subjecting them to the foulest abuse which the tongue of man could utter, he would order them to be beheaded, or else to be bound to a long, thin board. When they were securely bound to this, the board would be bent back until it described an arc, then, suddenly released. The force of the spring would break the victim's back and all his bones. Or men were tied to horses' tails and dragged over the plain until they died, or were thrust into a deep, dank, stinking dungeon to perish of hunger and be devoured by the rats. The king was a terrible man, and they were terrible times to live in, but more terrible still was the German queen. She was wicked beyond belief and she taught the king his cruel ways.

But came a time when he roused even his own uncles against him.

23

Some say that they numbered twelve, though others assert that there were thirty. Be that as it may, they revolted. They gathered their armies about them and marched on the castle, intending to conquer it and to take Popiel prisoner. The watch, standing on the tower, saw them from afar, a goodly array, led by powerful princes. But Chwastek gathered his defenders together and prepared for battle. The draw-bridges were raised, the fire was kindled and brought to the greatest possible heat, to heat the oil, provisions were hastily got in, pillaged, as a matter of course, from the townspeople. When the attacking forces tried to storm the castle, all Chwastek's defences went into action. It is impossible to tell how many men were killed. But the red-haired German woman was continually whispering into Popiel's ear, urging him to make peace, to promise freedom to the people, and to invite his uncles to a banquet within the castle, and she assured him that she would help him to get rid of them for ever.

So Chwastek did as she bade him. He performed a comedy. He wept, and, with doleful and contrite mien, swore that it broke his heart to see so much noble blood spilt, and so many good people killed. He said he was sorry for his sins, and he promised to reform. He promised to feed the hungry, he promised to care for the sick and aged, he promised to be a father to the orphan and a support to the widow. He promised everything, peace, plenty, all they desired. To his uncles he was humble and submissive. He invited them, if they would deign to honour his board, to a banquet within his castle. He would do what they wished, but he earnestly prayed that they would grace his table with their presence. They believed him and they accepted. They concluded peace and poured water over their swords. They swore oaths to their gods, oaths which it was a great sin to break, although theirs were pagan gods, for they were not Christians in those days.

The banquet was prepared. Whole sheep, hogs and wild boar were roasted on the spit. Strange mixtures of meat, sweets and spices were boiled in saffron, fried in butter and honey; sauces were concocted from currants, from the juices of herbs, from all different manner of ingredients. Besides e meat there were birds in great quantity, grouse, black-cock, duck, geese, a prepared in the most wonderful ways, even to seeming alive on the table. Wi there were, foreign, rich wines, malmsey and petercyment and mead, home ewed mead, made by the hand of the Queen herself.

In the great banqueting hall, the tables were groaning. Fresh rushes
had been laid on the stone-flagged floor, sweet, aromatic herbs were burn-
ing, and the light of the torches cast shadows on the arras-covered walls.
These arrases had been worked by the Queen and her ladies in their leisure
hours and they were worked with many fantastic scenes and bold colours
mingled with one another. They, except for the long tables and rude
benches, were the sole adorment of the high, vaulted banqueting-hall. All
the uncles were delighted and not one of them had any suspicion that all
was not well. The atmosphere was cheerful and the fare was excellent.
The uncles ate copiously and drank deep. Music, played by trumpeters,
gaily reflected the mood of the revellers. Chwastek himself was beaming
with happiness. His wife, richly dressed, sparkling with jewels, was as
beautiful and as sweet as an angel. Her red hair was braided with pearls,
there was a circlet on her white brow, of green, opalescent stones, which
caught and reflected the light of her strange, green eyes. She was dressed
in a tight-fitting gown of white velvet which revealed every curve of her
beautiful, lithe body, and emphasised the feline grace of her every movement. Her little waist, too, was encircled with gems and her fingers were
heavy with them. Yes, she was beautiful, but evil; and a man in his
sober senses, looking into her eyes, would have felt his blood run cold, as
though a basilisk had struck him. And had any man ventured boldly to
kiss those red lips, which looked so warm and enticing, he would have
drawn back appalled, for they were cold, cold as ice and hard as stone,
and tasting of death.

The company was merry, and they heeded not the evil glint of the
Queen's eyes, nor perceived that she bit her lip impatiently from time to
time. They only saw that she was beautiful, that she smiled upon them
and that she plied them with food and drink. Many were the compli-
ments which she received, and many were the half-joking, half-envious
allusions to her husband's good fortune in possessing such a treasure. As
the guests grew merrier and more fuddled, the Queen became more
gracious and more smiling and a look of triumph came into her eyes, as
they vociferously acclaimed Popiel and his Queen as the best sovereigns
in the world. The red-haired German rose to her feet and said: "Dear
Borns and Uncles, I desire you to grant me one boon. I pray you, drink
a toast with me, which I myself will pour into your goblets." And she

poured the rich, deep gold mead into each man's goblet, mead which she herself had brewed according to a secret known only in her family. She walked slowly round the table, holding the chased ewer aloft, moving smoothly and gracefully, conscious of her beauty. As she paused beside each guest, letting the golden mead trickle slowly into the goblet, she murmured some charming individual compliment. When all the uncles had been served, they rose as one man and drank the toast which the Queen proposed: "To eternal peace." They quaffed it at one draught, not a drop remained in the goblets.

Old Mszczuj was the first to feel the effects of the poison which he had taken. Seized with a searing, gnawing pain, he rose suddenly from the table crying: "Treachery"! He stumbled towards the wall where hung his battleaxe, and made frantic efforts to seize it, his hands groping along the wall like those of a blind man. Then, without warning, he fell heavily to the ground, dead. Then Bozywoj felt the poison tearing at his vittals. He drew his dagger and tried to thrust it into Chwastek's breast, but the dagger fell from his nerveless fingers and in a moment he too, was dead. The other guests were terrified, they clutched at their hearts, they gaped at the King and Queen, still hardly able to believe what had befallen them, still unable to grasp the extent of the treachery which had been practised upon them. They tried to rise, overturning the benches upon which they sat, but one by one they fell to the ground, where they lay groaning and writhing on the stone flags of the banqueting hall. And Chwastek stood up and shouted: "I promised you eternal peace; now you have eternal peace." And he laughed, and his German red-haired woman laughed, and their laughter echoed through the castle. They laughed as the uncles groaned and cried out, they laughed as the uncles cursed them, they laughed as the uncles died, one by one, and all their knights with them. Horrible was that laughter amid death, amid the curses and groans of the dying, amid the death-rattle of so many men. Horrible was that laughter ringing through the banqueting hall, which was the scene of such suffering, horrible was that laughter amid the dead, whose bodies were growing rigid already in the ungainly postures of a violent end. Horrible was the laughter of Popiel and his red-haired German wife.

The last uncle was dead, and the royal couple looked at each other in silent triumph. There was momentary silence, then voices were heard without, crying out in fear. Then the clatter of feet, fleeing in all haste.

As the last uncle had drawn his last breath, out of the Goplo lake had appeared myriads of mice, which advanced straight towards the castle. The sight of them terrified the servants and the soldiery who fled in all directions at their approach. The mice, in orderly array, swept up the approaches to the castle, over the drawbridge, through the court yard and into the banqueting hall. There, they halted not, but made straight for the King and Queen. They were horrible, fearsome creatures, grey, wet, disgusting, with their little pink eyes glistening and their little, fat bodies jostling one another. Their very whiskers seemed to bristle and it was as though their lips were curled back in a snarl to reveal their sharp, pointed teeth. There was a nauseating stench emanating from them, a stench of dampness, of rottenness and of death. Still they came forward and the royal couple stared at them as though transfixed. Suddenly the Queen screamed and, pulling her husband after her, ran to the tower which adjoined the banqueting hall. They shut the heavy oak doors behind them, thinking that they were safe. But the sound of gnawing was heard, gentle at first and then louder and more insistent until the oak doors shook and then—a hole appeared through which a grey body leapt. Then another, and another, and soon hundreds had rushed through the breach they made in the door. Popiel and his wife rushed in terror up the spiral stairs and shut themselves in yet another room, but the mice followed them, and ate their way through the door of that chamber like locusts. Now there were hundreds, thousands, millions. Sounds of a fearsome struggle could be heard as the wretched King and Queen battled with their loathsome attackers. Popiel killed hundreds of the mice, but it was of no avail, there were more and ever more of the revolting creatures. The courtiers and soldiers were huddled together outside, listening in terror to the shrieks of rage and despair which came from the tower. Screams for help grew louder and more desperate, but no one had the courage to move, no one had the courage to enter the castle. Howls of pain, horrible to hear, were soon succeeded by whimpering and groaning, which was even more blood curdling. And mingled with these sounds were excited squeaks and the scampering of millions of little feet. Then quiet—deathly, horrible quiet. After a short while the myriads of mice streamed out of the tower, through the banqueting hall, out through the court-yard, past the soldiers and courtiers who were frozen with terror, and back to the Lake of Goplo, where they disappeared into its waters.

It was not until some days later that the first brave men dared to enter the castle. They did so with trepidation and very, very warily. When they entered the banqueting hall, they found the bodies of Popiel's uncles, untouched, as they had died. But in the tower they found only the garments and jewels of Popiel and his Queen. Nothing more. The mice had eaten Popiel and his wife. They had eaten them because they were wicked, because they harmed the people over whom they reigned, because they were treacherous, because they laughed when the uncles lay dying in agony from the poison which they had received at the hands of the red-haired Queen. They ate the King and Queen, and not a trace of their bodies remained, in the Tower of the Mice, upon which we may stand to-day.

The castle of Kruszwica stood empty. There was no King. The reign was ended, and fear fell from the people. The mice had eaten Popiel and they had eaten his wicked red-haired German Queen.

THE LEGEND OF KRAKUS, WHO SLEW THE DRAGON

ON the River Vistula, there stands a hill now known as the Wawel Hill. On that hill stands to-day a beautiful and ancient castle, and a Cathedral in which are buried the Kings of Poland. Below, nestling, as it were, under its protecting shadow, lies the city of Krakow, the ancient capital of Poland. It is a beautiful city, whose very stones seem to speak of ancient glory and heroic deeds.

Long, long ago there was no castle on the Wawel Hill, only rocks and trees. There was no city of Krakow, but a small settlement of wooden huts inhabited by peaceful people who tilled the land and plied their trade, and prospered.

In the side of the Wawel Hill was a deep, dark cave. It had a forbidding look, and the entrance was overgrown with tall, rank weeds. No man had ever ventured inside that cave, and some said that a fearsome dragon lived within it. This was disbelieved by the younger generation, but old men said that they had heard their fathers tell of a dragon who slept in the cave, and no man must dare to waken it, or there would be dire consequences for them all.

But some of the youths determined to explore the cave and put an end of such foolish talk. What harm could come to them?—they argued. Dragons were all very fine for old men to believe in, but people with up-to-date ideas knew that such things simply did not exist.

So a band of five or six youths, armed with torches and flints with which to light their way into the dark recesses of the cave, set out to climb the side of the hill. They were warned against their enterprise by their elders, but they heeded not the warning. When they reached the entrance to the cave they halted and peered inside, trying to discern something in the darkness. They could see nothing. It was not a pleasant place, the weeds were thick and clung about their legs, the air was dank and foul and the whole place felt evil. Even the stoutest heart quailed and the boys began to look at one another doubtfully. But they were ashamed of their fears and they decided to go in. They lit their torches in silence, and one by one stepped carefully into the darkness. The cave was long and narrow and the light of the torches threw fantastic shadows on the walls. It seemed to the youths, as they advanced, that they could hear a deep and regular breathing, but they still went on.

Suddenly, a few paces in front of them they saw a large, heaving mass. It seemed to be of a greenish colour and covered with scales. Not waiting to see any more, the boys turned and fled towards the entrance of the cave. Behind them, they could hear a roaring and a bellowing and they could feel hot breath upon their backs as they ran. They did not pause at the entrance to the cave, but plunged on down the hill, stumbling in their haste. It was only when they reached the bottom of the hill that they dared to look back at the entrance of the cave. Any hopes they may have had, that their imagination had tricked them, were dispelled. There, at the entrance of the cave, stretching forth its hideous head, showing its long, sharp teeth and evil, flashing eyes, was the dragon. It waved its head slowly from side to side, let out a blood-curdling bellow and started to come down the hill-side.

It made its way towards a herd of grazing cattle which fled in terror at its approach. But the dragon was nimbler than they and, seizing one of the unfortunate beasts, it carried it back into the cave. The people looked on, appalled. Mothers clasped their children to their breasts. Men looked to their axes, and the boys who had woken the dragon slunk away, terrified by what they had done.

From that day, the people knew no peace. Daily the dragon appeared and carried off a victim. Sometimes a child, sometimes a sheep, sometimes even a grown man. Attempts were made to kill the dragon. Men banded themselves together, armed with axes, and lay in wait for it. But no axe could penetrate those strong scales, no blow could be struck, strong enough to harm the dragon. Many men died in a brave attempt to rid their country of this terrible curse, but in vain. In the village lived a man named Krakus, who was wise and learned. Men often came to him to ask his advice if they were sick or in trouble, and he was always ready with a remedy or good advice. Some said that he was magician, for he mixed draughts for the sick, or gave them herbs. But Krakus was not a magician; he was wiser than his fellows and had made experiments of different kinds with herbs and spices. Now, in this dire distress, Krakus' advice was sought again.

Perhaps he could find some way of destroying the dragon, or at least he might be able to put it to sleep again. Krakus pondered for a long time, stroking his chin and murmuring to himself. Then he asked them to bring him a young sheep, a fat, tender beast. He then turned to his jars, of which he kept a goodly number in his house, and started to mix a thick, yellow paste from the contents of one of them with the addition of water. The paste had a foetid, unpleasant smell, but, as soon as the sheep was brought, Krakus smeared it all over the animal. Then, quickly carrying it up the hill, he advanced as far as the mouth of the cave and threw the sheep inside.

There were a few moments of silent suspense. Then the dragon, roaring and bellowing, rushed down the hill to the Vistula. The sheep had been smeared with sulphur and the dragon had a terrible fire within, and a terrible thirst. When it reached the Vistula, it drank and it drank. Krakus and the people watched anxiously from the bank, hoping, and yet not daring to hope, for release from their suffering. The dragon began to swell, but still it drank and still it swelled. It went on drinking till suddenly there was a great explosion, and the dragon burst.

Great was the rejoicing at the death of the dragon. The people, impressed by the wisdom of Krakus, invited him to rule over them, and they built a stronghold on the Wawel Hill, now that they could scale its slopes without fear. The country prospered under the rule of Krakus and a city grew up around the hill which was called Krakow, in honour of Krakus.

When Krakus died, the people gave him a magnificent burial, and erected a mound over his tomb which can be seen to this day. The people brought earth with their own hands to the mound, and it has endured through all the centuries since its erection, a lasting monument to the love of the people for a wise and brave Prince.

THE LEGEND OF WANDA, WHO DROWNED HERSELF, RATHER THAN MARRY A GERMAN

KRAKUS had three children, two sons and one daughter. His elder son should have ruled when Krakus died, but he was slain by his younger brother, who coveted power for himself. But the people was angered by such wickedness, and they banished the murderer from their country for ever.

So the daughter of Krakus became the ruler of the country. Her name was Wanda, and she was very beautiful and, although she was but a young girl when she became Queen, she had wisdom and understanding far beyond her years. She loved her country very dearly and she ruled wisely and justly over the people who looked upon her with the greatest love and respect.

With all her qualities, her beauty and her wisdom, many princes sought to marry her, but Wanda would accept none of them, for she had not yet found one who was pleasing in her sight and who would help her to rule wisely and well over her beloved country. Poland was dear to Wanda, above all else, and she spared no effort to make her people happy. She waged war against aggressors who tried to invade her country, herself leading her soldiers in the battlefield. Her presence inspired them to defeat many foes.

Wanda's fame spread far and wide, and even a German Prince, named Rytigier, heard of her beauty, her valour and, what was even more attractive to him, he heard that the lands of Poland were fruitful and rich. He therefore sent messengers with a letter to Wanda. The messengers were received at Wanda's court with courtesy and hospitality, as was always the custom in Poland. It was noticed that they were rough, uncivilised men who seemed surprised at the luxury and comfort of Wanda's Court. After they had rested and changed their apparel, they were ushered into Wanda's presence. Although they made their obeisance before her, with seeming respect, they looked about them with an air of appraising the value of everything they saw before them, as though it would soon be theirs.

Wanda read the letter and turned deathly pale. The contents were clear enough: Rytigier asked for her hand in marriage, stipulating that as her dowry she should bring him the lands of Poland, and threatening war in the event of a refusal. Now Rytigier had a very powerful army, famed all over Europe as the strongest and best equiped of any prince. Wanda's army, on the other hand, had lost heavily in recent wars. To accept Rytigier's proposal of marriage was unthinkable. Wanda could not, would not subject her country to German rule. She looked at the two messengers and shuddered. Cruelty and rapacity were written plainly in their faces; and these, thought Wanda, were typical Germans. To wage war might be fatal with the armies so ill-matched. Defeat at the hands of the Germans would certainly bring the cruellest possible reprisals to the Poles. But, in a firm voice, Wanda made her answer. She refused to surrender herself and her country to the Germans. She had made her decision. Wanda would sacrifice her life for Poland.

She retired to her own appartments and there prayed to the gods that they would grant Poland freedom from the Germans in return for her sacrificing her life. Her prayer was granted, and Wanda threw herself into the Vistula. When her body was recovered, she was buried with all honours, and a mound was raised to her memory beside that of her father, Krakus.

The story of Wanda is known in Poland, to every Polish child, and her memory is respected and cherished as the brave Polish woman who died rather than give herself and her country to a German.

THE LEGEND OF THE PIASTS

LONG ago, in the town of Gniezno (which in old Slavonic means "nest") a great banquet was in preparation. The occasion was the "shearing" of the Prince's two sons. This ceremony was a pagan one, customary among the Slavs, for they were still pagans in those days. When a Slav boy reached the age of seven years, he had his hair shorn for the first time and had a name conferred upon him. The occasion was one for great rejoicing and feasting and many guests were invited. It was usual for the most honoured guest to perform the "shearing" ceremony himself.

So the city of Gniezno was bustling with movement, for many guests had been bidden to the banquet and some came from without the city. The citizens, dressed in their bravest apparel, thronged the streets. Many gorgeously arrayed princes, riding richly caparisoned horses and followed by knights as gaily clad as themselves, came from neighbouring states. They were greeted at the city gates with fanfares of trumpets and addresses of welcome from the City Fathers. Then they rode on through the streets, gaped at by an admiring crowd, and wound their way up the hill to the castle where the Prince himself received them, bowing low, and assuring them that all he possessed, unworthy as it might be, was theirs. Then he led his guests to within the castle and himself saw to it that they lacked nothing for their rest and refreshment.

Meanwhile two travellers, weary, and travel-stained, arrived at the gates of the city. They sought admission, but the guards were unwilling to allow them in. They asked the wanderers if they had been invited to the banquet which the Prince was giving for his sons, and on hearing that they had not, they abused them, calling them thieves, accusing them of wishing to harm the city, of intending to hurt the two young princes. The two travellers protested their innocence and begged to be allowed to rest for a while within the city. But the guards were adamant and turned them away with rough words. The people too, were angered, and started to throw stones at the unknown travellers who sought to enter their city at such a time. The two wanderers turned away, sad, disappointed and weary.

They walked away from Gniezno and, since God directed their steps, they came upon a small and humble cottage. It was built of mud-bricks, covered with thatch and surrounded by a modest garden in which grew a few vegetables. In front of the cottage stood a man, poorly clad, but with a strong, healthy look and a handsome, open countenance. He appeared to be in early middle-age and was well-knit and broad of shoulders, and his hair and beard were fair. Beside him stood a lad of some seven years, a hardy, fearless youngster, whose golden hair fell in curls to his shoulders and whose blue eyes looked wonderingly at the strangers.

The man, noticing the weariness of the travellers, approached them. His manner was simple and dignified, with nothing of servility in it. He asked them if they would rest a while within his cottage, assuring them that they were welcome, though the cottage was but small and poor. They accepted most willingly and, entering the cottage, said: "Rejoice truly that we have come! May you gain plenty, and honour and glory for your progeny."

The owner of the cottage was ploughman to the Prince, and his name was Piast. His wife's name was Rzepicha, which means "Little Turnip." This does not signify that she was ugly, or common. No, it meant that she was healthy and good, for men in those days lived chiefly on bread and turnips, which were considered most wholesome fare. There is to this day, among the country people of Poland, an expression "healthy as a turnip." So her name was rather a compliment to Piast's wife, and she was deserving of it. For she was tall, beautifully built and strong. She kept her modest cottage spotless, so that the earth floor was as clean as the floors in the Prince's castle, if not cleaner. She baked the best bread of any wife for miles around, and she was pleasant, with all the wifely virtues. Piast was considered a fortunate man. Now she hastened forward to welcome her unknown guests, apologising for the inadequacy of the cottage and the lack of fine foods for them. She brought them milk and new-baked bread and bade her son wait upon them. They satisfied their hunger, and feeling refreshed, fell to talking to the hospitable Piast and Rzepicha. The couple conversed on many diverse themes and showed so much wisdom that the travellers knew they had found the man they sought; and they resolved to carry out the mission which they had been sent to perform, and which was known only to themselves.

They asked Piast if he could give them something to drink other than milk, and he replied: "Indeed, I have a keg of fermented beer, which I have been keeping for the 'shearing' of my son; it is the only one I have. But what of that? Drink it, if you will." He had resolved to celebrate the "shearing" of his son at the same time as the Prince, for he was a poor man and he counted on the largesse, which his master would distribute among his people on this occasion, to provide for this. He intended to invite a few friends, not to a banquet, but to a simple supper. He had fattened the piglet to regale his friends.

The travellers told Piast to pour out the beer, because they knew that it would not decrease in quantity by their drinking it, but rather increase. It did so, and became so abundant that it filled all the vessels which Rzepicha could borrow, and it became of such a rich quality as is only served at a Prince's banquet. And the meat of the piglet, too, was cut up, and they say that it filled ten dishes and was so succulent that none had ever tasted the like. Piast and Rzepicha, seeing this miracle, thought that it must augur something very extraordinary for their son. They wished to invite the Prince and his companions to the "shearing," but they dared not until their guests advised them most strongly to do so. So the Prince and his companions were invited by the ploughman Piast. And the Prince by no means thought that he was conferring a great honour upon his ploughman by sitting at his board. In those days, Princes were not so great, nor had they such pride and arrogance as they had in later times, and they were not surrounded by such servile courtiers as those who praised their successors and pandered to their whims.

Piast and Rzepicha therefore prepared the banquet, for such it had now become, and the little house was cleaned and scrubbed, rushes were laid on the floor, bread was baked and the piglet's meat cooked. It was a great occasion for the good couple, and Rzepicha was proud when the Prince praised her bread and her home, and expressed pleasure at the good looks of her son. He himself, as the most honoured guest, performed the ceremony of shearing the boy's head. I cannot deny that Rzepicha wept a few furtive tears at the sight of her boy's golden curls being shorn. What mother would not? For she had been proud of those curls, and had loved to tend them, and had delighted to stroke them when the boy had sat at her feet or on her knees. But she was happy too, that her son was now growing up to be a youth, for after the "shearing" the boy was no longer considered a child, and he started the education which was to fit him for the duties of a man. The son of Piast and Rzepicha was given the name Ziemowit, as an augury of his future fate.

After this ceremony had taken place, young Ziemowit, son of Piast, grew in strength and progressed from day to day, and became a knight of fair fame and renown. When Popiel disappeared from the country— they say that he suffered much persecution from the mice—the son of that Piast who had been the hospitable host of angels, and whose cottage had received a Prince, was made ruler and he won great glory for himself, and the boundaries of his kingdom spread further than ever before. After him reigned Leszek, his son, who rivalled his father in exploits and bravery. After the death of Leszek his son, Ziemomysl ruled. Thus was the dynasty of the Piasts established.

THE LEGEND OF MIESZKO, WHO RECOVERED HIS SIGHT AND MARRIED DOMBROWKA

ZIEMOMYSL of Poland had a son, Mieszko, who became great and famous and was the first Prince of Poland to be known by a foreign name. He is referred to in a document of the times as Dago. He also Christianised Poland.

Mieszko was born blind. This was a terrible sorrow to his parents, the more so because he was a beautiful and intelligent child, with affectionate, winning ways. He had wonderful eyes, of a clear, pale grey and no man could tell that they were sightless until, looking closely, he would notice the lack of life in them as the boy stared emptily before him. Mieszko could not run about like other lads, nor play at hunting, nor at war, so he would sit beside his mother and fondle the ears of his dog, while he listened with rapt attention to the stories which she told him. Stories of the brave deeds of his father and grandfather, of how his ancestor, Piast the ploughman, had given shelter and hospitality to two angels, of how the wicked King Popiel and his Queen had been eaten by the mice, of how Gniezno came to be built. Mieszko would never tire of these tales (though he knew them all by heart), and would always beg to be told them again, listening intently and even correcting his mother if she altered the wording, be it ever so slightly.

When Mieszko's seventh birthday approached his father called together the councillors and dignitaries of the state and consulted them regarding the great banquet which should, according to custom, take place in honour of his son. Ziemomysl was loath to have such a ceremony for his blind boy, for he felt ashamed and deeply grieved that his son was so afflicted. But the councillors prevailed upon him, and the ceremony was arranged.

Mieszko was quite excited about the banquet, for it would be a change for him. There would be music, and he loved music. He would hear the laughter and merriment of the guests, and he would be allowed to taste mead, for his father had promised him this. So he looked forward to the great day and was somewhat less melancholy than was his wont.

41

When the time came to dress him for the banquet, his old nurse found him almost high-spirited. He repeatedly told her that he was sure that something wonderful was going to happen. At last he was ready and entered the great hall of the castle, his mother leading him by the hand. He was dressed in a tunic of white velvet and his hose were laced up with gold. A golden circlet was on his brow and delicate features. As he was led in by his mother, a murmur of admiration mingled with pity arose for the beautiful, sightless boy. They led him to a chair, where he sat in perfect silence, listening to the music. Ziemomysl watched him for a while, but such a feeling of sadness gripped him, that he turned away from the revellers and sat apart.

Meanwhile there was dancing. The music of the lutes and cymbals was joyous and sweet. The dancers, moving with graceful formality, made an ever-changing pattern of bright colours. Sometimes the dancers clapped their hands in time to the music, at others a singer's voice would be raised in accompaniment. Suddenly, one of the ladies noticed that Mieszko was standing up, staring at the dancers with an expression of the greatest delight on his generally expressionless face. She left the dance and glided up to him. The boy looked up at her with a joyous smile. "I can see," he whispered. Mieszko's mother came hurrying up, for her mother's instinct had told her that something was happening to her son. At a glance she realised the truth, and threw her arms around Mieszko, clasping him to her breast. Some of the courtiers ran to tell Ziemomysl. They found him quite alone, sitting with his head in his hands, sadly thinking of his boy. "Sir," they told him, "your son can see." Ziemomysl looked up sharply, "What say you"? he enquired of them. They repeated their assertion, but Ziemomysl would not believe them; he even grew angry at their constant reiterations that Mieszko could see. "Do not trifle with a father's feelings: the boy is blind and will always be so," he said angrily. But then his wife came to him, laughing and crying at the same time, and threw herself on his breast. "Mieszko can see, dearest love," she said, "Come, I will show you." And she led him by the hand to where the boy stood. Mieszko recognised his father and called him by name, as he did many other people though he had not seen them before. Then Ziemomysl believed that his son was cured; and great was his joy, and great the rejoicing of all those present. Dancing was renewed with great vigour, the banquet was the occasion for drinking the health of young Mieszko many times, and he replied by drinking the healths of the company in his first draught of mead, after which he fell asleep and was put to bed.

This miraculous cure profoundly moved Ziemomysl and all his court. The Prince asked some old, wise men who were about the palace what, in their opinion, was the significance of this occurrence. Had it some special meaning? Was Mieszko destined to play a great part in the history of his country? The wise old men were puzzled, and pondered the question profoundly, till at last one of them, older and wiser than the rest, gave the following explanation. The blindness which had afflicted Mieszko was symbolic of the blindness which afflicted Poland. Until his coming, Poland had been blind, but through Mieszko she would see, and be enlightened and raised above other nations. This answer remained a mystery to Ziemomysl, who was never able to interpret it. But it happened as the wise old man had foretold.

After he had regained his sight, Mieszko began his education as a knight and as a prince. He grew up strong and fearless, he excelled in all manner of exercise and he was gentle and wise. He had understanding and intuition, rare in a young man, which remained with him, perhaps, from the sad days of his blindness which he never forgot. He was a good and dutiful son, and when his father died, he wept over him and buried him with the greatest honours.

Then Mieszko reigned in the place of his father, from the year 960, and he was a brave Prince. He fought many wars against aggressive neighbours who tried to invade Poland, and he defeated them all. He even threw them back and occupied their lands, and Poland grew into a strong, united country under his rule. But he was still a pagan and, according to pagan custom, he took unto himself seven wives.

Then he fell in love with Dombrowka, who was a Czech princess and a good Christian. She was beautiful and good, and Mieszko ardently wished to marry her. Dombrowka returned the love of Mieszko, but she refused to accept him unless he would renounce paganism and his seven wives and become a Christian like herself. Mieszko hesitated for a while, but his love for Dombrowka overcame all other considerations, and he proclaimed his readiness to become a Christian. He renounced his seven wives and prepared himself to embrace his new faith. The Czech princess herself came to Poland, as the recognised Queen of Poland, but she came with a splendid retinue of bishops and priests, and refused to accept Mieszko as her true husband until he should be baptised. But she herself instructed him, and under her tuition, Mieszko slowly but surely learned the doctrines of the Christian faith, until at last he was ready to be received into the Church. His baptism took place with great ceremony, in that very hall in which, many years before, he had recovered his sight.

All Poland followed the example of the King, and embraced the Christian faith, through the influence of Dombrowka. Thus were fulfilled the predictions of the wise old man, who said that Mieszko's blindness was a symbol of the blindness of Poland, which until then had been living in the errors of paganism, but which, under the influence of Mieszko and his wife, saw the light of the true worship of God, and thus became a truly great and enlightened nation.

THE LEGEND OF ADALBERT, THE PATRON SAINT OF POLAND

TOWARDS the end of the 10th century, the Bishop of Prague, Adalbert, was invited by King Boleslaw of Poland to convert the Prussians, who were a pagan tribe living north of Poland. Bishop Adalbert accordingly set out with a few monks to preach the gospel to the Prussians.

As he approached the first Prussian settlement, which could be seen, a large cluster of huts, some distance away, he noticed a small cottage standing among trees, quite alone. He was about to enquire of his monks if they knew to whom it belonged, when the owner, a poor widow, came forth and offered the Bishop rest and refreshment within her humble dwelling. The Bishop declined, however, saying that he must press on, for it was growing late, though he accepted a cup of milk from the woman and gave her his blessing. He asked if she were not afraid to live so near the settlement of a wild and pagan tribe, but she replied that she was so poor, that they did not molest her, for, she added, the Prussians were a grasping people and she begged the Bishop that he would beware of them.

The little party continued, and soon reached the edge of the Prussian settlement. The tribesmen came out, heavily armed, and stared at the travellers, making threatening gestures and shouting. The Bishop, undaunted, held up his Cross, which was inlaid with precious stones. But this did not have the effect on the Prussians which he had hoped. Instead of being filled with reverence for the holy symbol of Christianity, the Prussians saw in it an object of value and they became greatly excited, and crowded round the Bishop, eagerly stretching forth their hands. Adalbert ordered them back in a firm voice, at the same time putting the Cross back in his bosom. This seemed to anger the Prussians and they pressed closer, seeking to tear the Cross from Adalbert's neck, round which it hung on a golden chain. The Bishop, in his effort to keep his Cross from irreverent, pagan hands, was badly manhandled, and all the efforts of the monks to protect him were in vain. The Prussians were becoming really angry, and one, bolder than the rest, lifted his club and struck Adalbert down. The other

45

pagans fell upon him, and in a few moments the Bishop had breathed his last. The monks fled in terror and returned to Gniezno, where they apprised Boleslaw of what had happened.

The Polish King was filled with anger and dismay. He shuddered to think what would happen to the body of Adalbert if it was left with the pagan Prussians, and it was, moreover, essential that the Bishop should receive Christian burial. He sent ambassadors to the Prussians at once, to demand the return of Adalbert's body. The Ambassadors accordingly set out, and, travelling as quickly as they could, soon reached the same spot where Adalbert had been put to death. The Prussians, who had watched their arrival with some curiosity, now came forward and, with some civility, enquired their will. The Ambassadors demanded the body of Adalbert, Bishop of Prague, in the name of King Boleslaw of Poland. But the Prussians were not going to part with their victim easily. They demanded the weight of the Bishop's body in gold, saying that otherwise they would not give it up. The Ambassadors had some gold, though in no great quantity, but they trusted in God to save the body of His servant from desecration. Two large baskets were brought, and placed each at one end of a long plank which lay athwart a log. Into one basket was bundled the body of Adalbert, into the other, the gold which the envoys had brought. But the weight of the body was far greater and the basket remained on the ground. The Ambassadors took off their jewels, chains, rings, ornaments, threw them all into the basket, but still there was not enough. Then, when all hope seemed lost, a poorly-clad woman timidly approached. It was the same widow who had given the Bishop a cup of milk as he had journeyed towards the Prussians. Now she came forward holding in her hand a tiny gold coin. It was the only treasure which the poor woman possessed and had been part of her dowry—the only part which remained to her. She placed it in the basket, very shyly, as though ashamed of her humble offering. The Prussians began to laugh. But their laughter changed to amazement when the basket containing the gold began to sink slowly down until it reached the level of that containing the Bishop's body, then it stayed quite still; the balance was exact. The Prussians were surprised, a little afraid, and deeply impressed. They soon became convinced that they were not all-powerful, as they had thought, and were converted.

But this is not the end of the story. For the Emperor Otto III, who was a Christian, wished to visit the tomb of Bishop St. Adalbert, for he had been canonised, and so, in the year 1000 A.D. there was a great Congress at Gniezno, and King Boleslaw solemnly received the Emperor. Now that same Otto III had received Boleslaw's father, Duke Mieszko I, as a vassal. But in Gniezno, as we tell elsewhere, he was received as an equal, and he did not hesitate to place his own crown upon the head of Boleslaw, and to present him with the lance of St. Maurice. A chronicler tells us that Gniezno was magnificent in those days as no other city and that silver and gold were common there, as baser metals in other countries. Boleslaw was the first crowned King of Poland and he made her a great country.

HOW THE EMPEROR OTTO VISITED GNIEZNO

IT is an incontestable fact that the Emperor Otto III visited Gniezno in the year 1000 A.D. There is no actual contemporary written record of the visit, but the story was handed down from father to son, and here it is.

Boleslaw the Brave was not yet King at the time. In the year 1000 he was still called Duke, but he was, nevertheless, a powerful prince. Now in his capital of Gniezno were laid the remains of St. Adalbert—or Wojciech as he is called in Poland—who in his life had been a saintly man and who had lost that life at the hands of the pagan Prussians.

It so happened that, not long after Wojciech's death, the year 1000 was born. A thousand years had passed since the birth of Christ. Man thought that the year 1000 would see the end of the world, and the Judgment Day, and many were afraid, for they had given way to sin. Pilgrimages were made, prayers were offered up, churches and monasteries were built and endowed, all in the hope that sins would be forgiven—if the world ended.

Otto III, Emperor of Germany and of the Holy Roman Empire, who had known Bishop Adalbert before his death, decided to make a pilgrimage to Gniezno, not only to pray for forgiveness at the tomb of the saint, but also to ascertain what manner of man was Duke Boleslaw. He had heard much of the Polish ruler, of his power, of his skill and daring as a warrior, of his wise rule. Otto was a young man, he was only twenty years of age, but he had been Emperor since his earliest childhood and he, like all men at the time, had matured young, so that he was a man of experience, despite his youth.

When Boleslaw heard of Otto's intention, he resolved to receive his guest—the most powerful prince in Europe—in a fitting manner. He wished to show his mighty neighbour that Poland was a great country and worthy of alliance with Germany.

As soon as the Emperor Otto reached the frontier, he was met by a large number of ecclesiastics; all dressed in ceremonial robes, and by many knights. These knights were mounted on powerful horses, and the excellence of their arms, the rich caparisoning of their horses, and the multitude

49

and diversity of their banners, filled the Emperor and his retinue with astonishment. They had heard tell of the fighting valour of the Poles, but they had expected fierce, wild warriors, armed but with the most primitive weapons and probably dressed in skins. And here were knights, with courtly bearing and polished manners, mounted and armed as well as those in the Emperor's train.

The knights guided the Emperor and his retinue through the lands which were unknown to them. A part of the country was wild and unpopulated, but those parts which were inhabited struck the visitors with their air of order and prosperity. The houses were well-built of wood, the fields were tilled and the beasts were tended and the people looked happy and peaceful. The Emperor Otto, a pious man, was well pleased to see that every village had its church, and in one of the larger villages, he expressed a wish to enter and pray. He dismounted accordingly and entered the wooden church. He was astonished at the beauty of the simple place of worship. The floor was strewn with rushes, on the walls were limned rough but colourful pictures representing scenes from the Life of Christ, the lamps were bright, flowers adorned the altar. Pious, loving hands had swept and garnished and made the little church a bright and beautiful place. The Emperor Otto began to feel respect as well as wonder for Poland.

As they proceeded on their way, they were joined by more and more knights with their mounted and armed attendants. They were well mounted, heavily armed, and richly attired. The Emperor thought that Boleslaw must indeed have a splendid army, that he must be a useful ally but a dangerous foe.

When they neared Gniezno, messengers spurred on to aprise the Duke of the Emperor's arrival. Boleslaw rode out of his capital to greet his powerful and illustrious guest. And behind him rode a retinue of knights larger and more splendid than that which had accompanied Otto thither.

The two princes exchanged greeting in solemn ceremony, each observing the other shrewdly. Boleslaw, several years older than Otto, was taller and more powerfully made. There was a moment's silence, then Boleslaw spoke a few words of greeting and compliment to his guest. Otto was astounded. So the Polish Duke spoke Latin! The German Emperor was a man of education, for his tutor had been Gerbert, the French Bishop who afterwards became Pope Sylvester II, and who was one of the best-educated men of his day. But Boleslaw, although he was famed as a warrior, had not neglected learning, and he was well able to converse with his guest.

They arrived at the gates of Gniezno. The capital was situated on a hill, and surrounded by strong wooden walls. At the gate, a great crowd had assembled to greet the guest. Otto dismounted, saying that he wished to accomplish the rest of the pilgrimage on foot. Hearing this, Boleslaw, also dismounting, ordered that red cloth should be laid in the streets through which the pilgrim should walk. After he had rested a short time and refreshed himself with a draught of cooling wine, the Emperor set out on the last stage of his pilgrimage to the grave of the holy St. Wojciech. Reverently, with clasped hands, he walked through the streets of the capital, silent, respectful crowds lined the streets, dressed in their finest attire, and were, the Emperor noticed out of the corner of his eye, more prosperous-looking than any townsmen that he had seen before.

When he came to the tomb of the Saint, he fell on his knees, and prayed long and fervently. The tomb, which was made of silver, richly adorned with precious stones and beautifully chased, shone in the light of a thousand candles.

When Otto had completed his prayers, Boleslaw invited him to his castle, which was large, strongly built of wood and had enormous rooms, many turrets, guardrooms and all the offices appertaining to a princely residence.

Otto was shown to his appartments, the furnishings of which were of surpassing richness. In a room adjoining that in which he was to sleep, was a huge basin made of silver, large enough for a man to step into. Attendants were filling it with warm water, richly perfumed. After he had bathed and changed his clothes, Otto was led to the banqueting hall. This was a long, high chamber, with a raftered ceiling. The walls were covered with arms and weapons of all kinds, coats of mail, richly wrought helmets, lances, spears and swords. Long oak tables and benches were placed in the centre and upon these were goblets and dishes of silver and gold. A great banquet began. Boleslaw, dressed with great splendour, glittering with jewels, did the honours with all the grace and charm for which the warrior prince was famous in his own country.

Cooked meats, spiced, fried in honey, game of every conceivable kind, fish cooked in wonderful sauces, sweets, spiced cakes, fruit, wines, mead and other most delicious and refreshing drinks, all made the eyes of the Germans open wide, and they fell to with a good will. At first, few sounds were to be heard except eating, drinking, smacking of lips, grunts of satisfaction and other noises whereby the German guests expressed their delight and enjoyment. They did full justice to the fare, and the Polish knights looked, in their turn, surprised and a little amused at such undisguised enjoyment of good food.

But when the appetites were satisfied, conversation began. There were some interpreters, who were called upon to help, but with the Emperor and Boleslaw, these were not necessary. They conversed quite amiably together in Latin. Otto asked many questions about Poland, which Boleslaw gladly answered. He told Otto about his army, about the produce of his country and about her riches.

When the banquet was ended, Boleslaw ordered the servants to strip the walls of the banqueting hall of all the rich weapons, and to gather together the gold and silver goblets and dishes, and to lay them at the feet of the Emperor whom he begged to accept this humble present.

The next day, there was a solemn High Mass in the church at Gniezno, attended by both princes. This was celebrated with great splendour, and fervent prayers were offered up for the illustrious guest who had come to the grave of the patron Saint of Poland. After the Mass, there was another banquet, and to the Emperor's great surprise, the banqueting hall, which had been stripped, was once more adorned with rich arms and the tables were covered with silver and gold. And at the end of the banquet, at which the fair was as splendid as ever, Boleslaw once more gave Otto all the arms and jewelled plate as a present.

The Emperor saw that here indeed was a neighbour whom it would be worth while to have as a friend. He wished in some way to repay the kindness and hospitality of his host, and in a way befitting to an Emperor. He therefore raised Gniezno to the dignity of an Archbishopric, so that the Polish clergy were no longer subject to the German clergy.

And he took the crown from his own head, and placed it upon that of Boleslaw saying: "Thou shalt be king." And thereafter Boleslaw was King of Poland, and was always known as King, though his solemn coronation took place twenty-five years later.

THE LEGEND OF BOLESLAW AND HIS KNIGHTS

WHEN King Boleslaw died, Poland lost a very able and brave ruler, one who had united her and made her into a really great country. But is Boleslaw lost to Poland? Some say no, for there is a legend about Boleslaw and his Knights, which I will tell you.

They say that Boleslaw, and his Knights who fought with him—for he was a great warrior and earned his title of The Brave by routing Poland's enemies—went into a mountain called Gevont. This mountain forms part of the Tatra, and its shape, as seen from a certain angle, is like the head of a sleeping knight. Within this mountain is a huge, dark cavern and there sleep King Boleslaw the Brave and hundreds of his knights. They are mounted on their horses, with their swords beside them and lances couched. And if Poland needs them, then someone must awake them, and they will ride forth to serve her. But once they have gone forth, they will never return.

The legend also tells that in olden days a blacksmith went every year to shoe the warriors' horses. This was a task which must be carried out in complete silence lest the warriors should awake and, thinking that the summons had come, ride forth. The blacksmith who performed the task received a piece of gold which was silently handed to him by the King himself, who sat silently on his charger near the entrance of the cave. No one knew whether the King slept or woke, for his movements were so smooth, so deliberate, that he was as a man in a trance. He always acknowledged the thanks of the blacksmith with a courtly inclination of the head, but none had ever beheld his eyes.

The task of shoeing the knights' horses had been handed down through the same family of blacksmiths from father to son for many generations. It was a much prized task and required unusual skill on account of the silence in which it had to be carried out. The danger of awakening the knights was impressed upon all those blacksmiths who undertook the task.

The shoeing was always performed at the same time of year, in the spring. One year, the old blacksmith who had performed it for thirty years was ill, and unable to leave his bed. He was very much distressed at this, but his son, a strong young man who had been helping his father in the smithy since he was a boy, assured him that he would carry out the task perfectly well. "I shall have to do it one day," he said, "so why not to-day? Be assured, Father, that I will not speak a word." The old man, still unconvinced and muttering about the irresponsibility of youth, tried to leave his bed, but the pain was too great for him to rise, and he was forced to lie down again and reluctantly allow his son to go, with many parting injunctions.

The young blacksmith started merrily off with his new horseshoes and his tools. His father had given him minute instructions where to light the fire with which to heat the shoes, and the order in which the knights' horses were to be shod, finishing with the King who was at the head of the array and nearest the entrance. When the young man arrived at the entrance to the cavern, he felt a little nervous at the unaccustomed darkness, but he soon overcame this and looked eagerly around him. There, motionless, clad in rich armour and armed with swords, battleaxes and lances, sat the knights astride of their chargers. They were big men, for the most part, with clear-cut features and fair hair. At their head was King Boleslaw, with his long hair and fierce, curling moustaches. Their chargers were heavy, powerful beasts, some covered in armour, some with only a breastplate and frontal piece, but all richly caparisoned. The young blacksmith, lost in contemplation, was forgetting his task, when one of the horses pawed the ground as if impatient. The fire was soon lit, the shoes heated and the work begun. It was a strange task, the shoeing of so many horses with their sleeping riders motionless astride them. The fire threw strange shadows on the walls of the cavern, making the knights' shadows dance and assume gigantic proportions. The young blacksmith had almost completed his task, he was shoeing the last horse, that of the King, when he dropped a red-hot horse-shoe on his foot. "Psiakrew!"* he cried, and, as he said it, the knights awoke. "What? what?" he heard on every side. "Did you call us? Answer, and we will come." But he answered not and remained completely silent. The knights, after some more muttering, went back to sleep. But as the blacksmith, after silently completing the shoeing of the King's horse, turned to go, he received a very sharp blow on the shoulders

---

* "Psiakrew"—a mild Polish swearword, meaning "Dog's blood."

accompanied by a painful prod lower down. King Boleslaw had not gone back to sleep, and instead of a gold piece, was giving the blacksmith a sound drubbing. The young man fled. But since that day, no one has ventured into the cavern, and the knights, with King Boleslaw, sleep undisturbed, waiting, waiting until they are called to fight for Poland for the last time.

THE STORY OF THE "RESURRECTED BROTHERS"

KING BOLESLAW the Brave was a great warrior, and he gathered about him many knights who followed him to war against Poland's enemies. These knights were brave men, hot-blooded and daring, and their deeds in war were famous throughout Poland. In times of peace, however, some of the knights were not content with the chase, or with tourneys, to give vent to their high spirits, and sometimes, though it was only very seldom, they would ride forth and attack parties of travellers and merchants, rob them and even, on occasion, kill them.

Now this was quite a usual occurrence in Germany, where the powerful were wont to increase their riches by robbing the weak. But in Poland such a practice was looked upon with disgust, and when reports of the knights' behaviour reached King Boleslaw, he was very angry. He wished for justice in his country, and for the weak to feel as secure as the strong. He wished his country to be safe for travellers, hospitable for strangers. He had made good roads in Poland, wishing to encourage merchants from abroad to come into the country, bringing the goods which were so necessary to her. Was Poland's prosperity, her peacefulness, nay, her very good name, to be injured by a few hot-headed, high-spirited knights?

King Boleslaw was very angry, and he issued a decree whereby he named death as the penalty for anyone who robbed or harmed a traveller. He was satisfied that this measure would put an end to such wicked ways.

But there were two young knights, brothers.

These two young men, and they were very young, not yet twenty, rode forth one day on a hunting expedition. They set out in great good spirits, hoping for a fine day's sport. But sport there was none. Either the beasts had betaken themselves to another part of the forest, or the wind was adverse, but never a quarry did they see all day. They were disappointed and fretful as they rode home, their young faces sullen, their smooth brows furrowed with frowns. Reaching the road, they perceived a small band of travellers approaching. Some elderly men on small horses, a large wagon drawn by oxen and driven by a stout-looking lad, and behind this, two heavily-laden camels, ridden by dusky, turbaned boys.

Eastern merchants! Going to the capital with rich merchandise, lovely silks, woven in fantastic colours and gorgeous patterns, precious spices and fine-wrought jewels. The King would be glad of these and would give much gold in return. The two brothers scowled at the little cavalcade. The younger, who was more hot-headed than his brother, said: "Here is sport for us, my brother; come, let us attack them!" Not heeding the King's commands, thinking not of the punishment, the knights rode at the party with all the speed they could muster, shouting ferociously. They scattered the frightened horsemen, pushed the lad off the cart, caused the camels to kick out and dislodge their riders, and generally created much confusion. It must be said that they took very little booty after this, only a few jewels which, they thought, would please certain fair maidens.

The scattered merchants reassembled. They assisted the lad to his feet, and found that he was bruised and shaken. With difficulty the camels were quieted, their loads readjusted, their riders soothed. The merchants were very surprised at what had happened, for they had heard that the roads of Poland were safe from robbers.

When they arrived in Gniezno, they were led before the King. Boleslaw questioned them closely on their journey, expressing the hope that they found the roads good and safe. The merchants told their story. They had been set upon by two young knights, and robbed, though of very little, and one of their servants had been hurt. King Boleslaw's brow grew black. He enquired where this had taken place, and ordered some of his guard to repair there at once and apprehend the two young knights.

The two offenders were feeling a little ashamed of themselves. Their hot temper had passed, and, being at heart brave men and true knights, they were very sorry for what they had done. When the guards came to take them to the King, their spirits sank and they became afraid. Now they remembered the King's decree and his anger against robbers. They were devoted to their sovereign, and would willingly have given their lives in his service, but they had been heedless, as youth so often is.

They arrived at the King's court at Gniezno and stood before Boleslaw. His countenance was terrible to behold. He addressed the two offenders: "You, felons, criminals, you have broken the law, you have robbed peace-

ful, unarmed merchants, you have hurt a defenceless lad. You are not worthy to live in our good realm of Poland; with your heads shall you pay for this. You shall die." All who heard the King's words were sore distressed, and grieved to see two strong, brave young men go to their death. But none dared to protest, for the King was terrible in his anger. The two young knights dared not ask for pardon; they knew that they would not obtain it. They allowed themselves to be led away in silence.

. . . .

A few years passed.

Boleslaw was once again preparing for war against Poland's enemies. He had summoned all his knights for the coming battle, and they had come to Gniezno joyfully, willingly, glad to give their services to Poland and their King. Boleslaw looked lovingly upon them, greeting each one in his turn as an old friend.

That evening there was a great banquet which was attended by the Queen. The knights conversed of this and that, recalling former campaigns and former comrades-in-arms, some of whom they would never see again.

Some one spoke of the young brothers, saying that it was a pity that such brave, strong lads should have thrown away their lives for a foolish prank.

Noticing that her husband seemed to share this regret, the Queen said to him: "Dost thou not regret these two young knights, my husband? Wouldst not be happy to see them alive once more?"

The King admitted that he would, that he would gladly set eyes upon them once more and let them fight for their country.

Then the Queen fell at her husband's feet.

"Unbeknown to thee, my Lord, I saved the lives of those two brothers. I caused them to be sent to a monastery, where they are even now expiating their sins. Wilt thou forgive them? Wilt thou permit them to fight for Poland?"

King Boleslaw was happy to hear what the Queen had to tell him, and raising her, he embraced her saying: "Thou art a good and merciful woman. May God reward thee for thy virtous heart."

Messengers were sent at once to the monastery in which the two brothers were living, performing menial tasks for the monks and passing much of their time in prayer. When they heard the tidings, they were filled with joy, and they hastened to court to throw themselves at the feet of the King and ask for foregiveness, and to thank the Queen, with all their hearts, for her intervention.

Everyone was happy to see them, and great was the rejoicing at court among the knights. The two brothers distinguished themselves in battle, and became Poland's two best-known warriors, always given the name, because of their strange fortune, of "The Resurrected Brothers."

THE TRUMPETER OF KRAKOW—AND THE LEGEND
OF SAMARKAND

IN Krakow, the ancient capital of Poland, there is a Church in the
Market Square. It is a tall, graceful building of pink brick, in the
Gothic style, with richly adorned walls inside. It has two towers, one
of which is a little higher than the other and more ornate. From the taller
tower a fanfare is played by a trumpeter, every hour. It is repeated four
times, but it always ends abruptly, on a broken note.

This is the story of the "Hejnal," as it is called.

From the tower of the Church, for centuries past, the Hejnal, or Hymn
to Our Lady (whose Church it is), was played by a trumpeter. He played
it four times—to the four winds—and he played it every hour. One day,
many, many years ago, as he played, the trumpeter saw in the distance a
cloud of dust which grew bigger with every passing moment. It was a large
army of Tatars galloping towards the city. These cruel invaders from the
east had more than once advanced to Krakow, nay, even farther, and they
had pillaged and burnt, looted and murdered and carried off the young
people to be slaves in their camps. The trumpeter was horror-stricken.
How could he warn the city, how could he convey to the people the approach
of danger and give them time to prepare their defence? There was only
one thing he could do. To go down into the town and spread the alarm
would be foolish, for it would waste precious minutes. He must play the
Hejnal, over and over. That would surely rouse the citizens, they would
certainly be aware of approaching danger. So he played, again and again.

At first the people of Krakow were puzzled. Why was the trumpeter
playing over and over? And with such loud urgency? But they quickly
realised that it was a warning and that from his lofty tower he had seen
danger approach. The soldiers sprang to arms and took up their stations on
the walls of the city. The burgesses ran to secure their houses and place
their wives and children behind locked doors. The apprentices seized their
arrows and their cross-bows, the artisans seized what tools they could lay
hands on, and they all marched to the defence of their city. Suddenly, the

sound of the Hejnal ceased abruptly. The notes had reached the ears of the Tatars as they approached, and their keen eyes had espied the figure of the trumpeter. As soon as they came within bow-shot, their leader, the surest marksman of them all, loosed his bow, and the deadly projectile lodged in the trumpeter's throat.

But his task was accomplished, and Krakow was saved. Thanks to his warning, the people were able to defend the city, and they inflicted a crushing defeat on the Tatars, killing one of their princes.

And since that day, the Hejnal has been broken off at the same note on which it was broken off by the Tatar arrow, in honour of the trumpeter who gave his life for the city.

That is the legend of the trumpeter of Krakow. Many historians, finding no documents to prove the story, asserted that it was not true, but that it was just a popular tale. They said that the Tatars had never fallen unexpectedly on the city of Krakow, and, if they had been Tatars why, in the annual pageant held to commemorate the event, were the "invaders" dressed in clothes which resembled rather those of far-eastern lands, than those of Crimea whence the Tatars came? But many people believed in their legend, affirming that there is always a foundation for legends and that a story which has been handed down for generations and which is known to a whole village or district, is more likely to be true than an account found on an ancient parchment in a dusty archive and written by the hand of one man alone.

These people may be right.

· · · · · · · ·

A Polish officer, a former student of Krakow University and a firm believer in the legend, was taken prisoner by the Russian army in 1939. After his release two years later he found himself, after some wandering, with others of the Polish army in Samarkand, the ancient capital of Tamerlane. Under its former name of Maracanda, the city had been destroyed by Alexander the Great, but centuries later, under Tamerlane, it had once more become a great and prosperous city. It has since declined, but the people, who are Muslims, recall their former greatness.

These people, living as they do in so remote a place, had heard little of Europe and its countries. But one country they knew: Lechistan—Poland.

They had greeted their guests of the Polish army with traditional oriental courtesy, calm and grave. But when they heard that these guests were from Lechistan, they betrayed signs of keen interest.

"You are truly the sons of Lechistan?" they asked.

"We are."

"And you are soldiers?"

"Yes."

Then, after a silence:

"You believe in God? The same God in which you believed long ago?"

"Yes, we do; we have priests; see, we wear crosses," and the soldiers drew forth small crosses from beneath their uniforms, crosses cut from a food tin, since there were no others.

The people of Samarkand looked upon these crosses with a strange joy. But the next question seemed strangely irrelevant.

"And you have trumpeters?"

"We have."

A silence, and then, shyly:

"We have a request to make to you. If you are from Lechistan, and soldiers, and you believe in your ancient God, and you have trumpeters, could you—could you ask those trumpeters to play to-morrow evening in the old market square? Opposite the Mosque where lie the ashes of Great Timur?"

The Polish soldiers agreed, puzzled, and they were still more puzzled by the enormous, silent crowd which had gathered in the square.

They played a reveille, they played regimental marches and at last they played the Hejnal. There was complete silence in the square, and in silence the people dispersed. It seemed that they were very happy, but they would not speak.

It was only a little later that the Poles learnt the reason for the strange request, and for the joy of the people. There is, it seems, a legend too, in Samarkand. And this was the story they heard.

Once, long ago, the people of Samarkand took part with the Tatars in one of the invasions of Poland. And they came to a city which, they say, was the same for Lechistan as Samarkand was for them. A capital, a very old, very rich city. And a holy city, for from one of the minarets a trumpeter called the people to prayer. The Tatars wished to take the city by surprise, but the trumpeter was able to raise the alarm before a Tatar arrow killed him, lodging in his throat. The city defended itself and the Tatars were defeated.

A Tatar prince was killed and the elders and priests, to whom a report of the campaign was faithfully given, pronounced that it was a punishment from Heaven, for having killed a man who was calling the people to prayer. And they predicted that Samarkand would lose her greatness, would lose her liberty. But yet prosperity would return, though not until trumpeters from Lechistan should play in the market square that same song which was cut short by the arrow of the Tatar.